D1806545

Life After Grief

Life After Grief

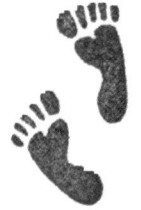

Janet Rosauer

ISBN: 1-890676-25-X

Library of Congress Catalog Card Number: 98-86807

Printed in the United States of America.
First Printing: August, 1998

01 00 99 98   6 5 4 3 2 1

Beaver's Pond Press

5125 Danen's Drive
Edina, MN 55439-1465

THIS BOOK IS DEDICATED:

To God, who gave me strength when I was exhausted,
showed me the light on gloomy days and gave me
wisdom and compassion to write this book.

《《《

To my loving husband, who put up with me and all my moods. Our
marriage survived more trials in eight years than most marriages do
in 50. Thank God you're my soulmate!

《《《

To my children, Jesse, Clint and Travis, for without
them this book would not be possible.

《《《

To my mother, who not only helped endless loving hours
with Clint and Jesse but also spent countless
hours editing this book.

《《《

To my dear niece Erin, who gave me those much
needed breaks from my sweet baby.

《《《

To the rest of my family and friends, who are always
there for me—especially my terrific sister Kathy,
whose ear I bent a few too many times.

《《《

To Jesse's and Clint's teachers and Washington County Services; also,
support groups in Washington County, Family Service St. Croix, The
Lissencephaly Network and Compassionate Friends.

《《《

To my internet friends, Jennifer, Rhonda, Karen, Tina, Colleen
and Kathy, who may not realize how much help they really were
on my sad and lonely days.

《《《

To Dr. William Dobyns, who was always very honest with us,
never sugarcoating Clint's problem; he gave above and
beyond what we'd ever expect from a doctor.

IN MEMORY OF:

My baby, Clint
My father in law, Frederick (Fritz) Rosauer
My good friend, Barb
Kaylen
Chevas
Duane
All our loved ones we miss so much

Chapter One

I don't remember much about my life before junior high age, except that I was very awkward and mostly a pest to my brother and sister. I wasn't close to Dave and Kathy, since they were five and four years older. Our relationship grew only after I graduated and moved out of our parents' house. I do remember my mother going through emotional turmoil while recovering from alcoholism, and my parents "discussing loudly" problems they needed to work out. Mom never had a relapse. She's been straight now for 25 years, and I still see us all as a nice happy-but-slightly-dysfunctional family.

With my brother going to college out of state, and my sister getting married and moving to California, I felt like an only child in high school. Except for the homework, I loved Mariner High School. It was the 1970s, and the school was new and very liberal. There were no permanent walls to separate the classes and we had a modular style scheduling. Modular scheduling was a bit confusing. It consisted of a six day schedule with 17 "mods" in a day each being 23 minutes long. I remember waking up every Monday morning trying to think which day it was: "Let's see...Friday was day 5, because I had biology, so today must be day 6 and I have phy ed, math...."

Most of my enjoyment in school centered around time with my friends. I could hardly wait to get out of class to meet my buddies across from the library in the annex—an open room supposedly made for studying. We'd sit at a large table and talk about stuff. Heaven forbid we'd ever talk about school work. Most of my friends were involved in theater or choir. These people were, and still are, the most creative bunch of individuals I've ever met.

After graduation, I felt as if I hadn't learned a thing from my high school years. Little did I know the things I *had* learned would become the most valuable assets in my life. One of my classes called "Little Lives," taught us how to discipline and teach toddlers.

One day we went on a field trip to Cambridge State Hospital for that class. This center was for the mentally and physically handicapped ranging from mild to the most severely challenged. When we arrived, they started the tour immediately. First they showed us the most severely handicapped. We walked into a large room where the young and old were just lying in beds.

The first person I saw had hydrocephalus. He was almost an adult and his head was larger than his body, so he couldn't even sit up. I remember thinking I can see why this poor man is institutionalized. How could any parent take care of a person like this?

Then they brought us to other rooms where the adults were higher functioning. These people were doing certain tasks based on their abilities. I couldn't understand why these people were in this facility. They appeared able to live and work in the real world. I'll never forget my experiences on that tour as long as I live. I'm sure things have changed considerably since the 70s, but the conditions were not something in which I'd ever want my child to live.

My mind wandered while on the bus heading back to school. I couldn't imagine what the parents went through, giving up their children to the state. I wondered what it must be like for those people back in the institution. Did they feel abandoned by their parents? Were they so young they didn't remember what family life was like? The ones that were practically vegetables—what was their existence like? Looking back on that day, I realize it was one of the turning points in my life. My parents did a good job showing me their strong faith in God, but after seeing those people I had questions and doubts. Would God do this to people? If so, why? Little did I know then how those questions would haunt me again 20 years later.

 # Chapter Two

During my senior year in high school I met a girl named Evey, and we became best friends during our first quarter at Lakewood Junior College. We took Abnormal Psychology class together in our second quarter. Since Evey worked at a group home for mentally disabled children, she was already somewhat knowledgeable with this class. We hated the way the teacher taught, since he spent most of the time writing each lecture on the blackboard instead of talking to us. One day, his lecture was about autism and he wrote that autism was actually a form of retardation. After reading this, Evey quickly raised her hand and stated, "There's new information on autism. You could be autistic, but not retarded at all."

You'd think she slapped him in the face! He cut her short and told her if she knew so much about autism maybe she should write a report on it for extra credit. We looked at each other with the same thought...not too pompous, is he?

Evey and I never completed the class. During that semester Evey's father became quite ill and passed away from leukemia. Because of this she missed a few too many classes and I couldn't get her to go back. I returned once, but without Evey there, the class was just too hard to stomach.

I'd never experienced a death in my family so the loss of Evey's father was quite enlightening. When she told me on the phone that he had died, I was sitting across from my own father in the living room. I just stared at him when she told me the news. My heart ached for her and I couldn't imagine what it would be like without my dad. When we got off the phone I ran to my dad and wrapped my arms around him and sobbed.

That evening I called and broke the news to all of our friends, so we could all go to the funeral together. I'd never been to a Jewish ceremony before and found it to be quite beautiful. The Jewish religion has seven days of mourning, and their family and friends gathered on and off at her mother's home during that time.

The following week, her mother went to Alaska for her job. Evey didn't want to be alone in that big place, so I offered to stay with her. This was my first real taste of being out on my own and I liked it. Since I knew college wasn't for me, I quit, got a full time job at a bank, and in January, 1979, moved out of my parents' house, when I was only 19.

This was the start of a new life for me, with a whole set of new responsibilities and learning experiences. I grew up fast and it caused me to look at my parents in a whole new light. I stopped thinking of them as dumb old mom and dad. Their rules and expectations finally made sense to me. But of course I broke all those rules at first. I'd stay up late on weeknights, then drag my sleep-deprived body out of bed in order to get to work on time. I wouldn't dare get to work late, since I was a morning teller, and had to open the drive-through window at 7:30 a.m. It only took a few weeks of sleep deprivation before I wised up and waited for the weekends.

Doing weekly cleaning was just another broken rule for me, until friends would stop by unexpectedly. This turned into a bad habit, and to this day I seem to wait until I can no longer stand the dirt or I find out company is coming. It's one big dream of mine to have enough money for a maid.

The summer after I moved out, my sister filed for divorce. She and her two little girls Erin and Heather had to move back in with our mom and dad until she found a new job at the school district. Kathy and I became much closer that year, going to parties and bars with my friends, and generally teaching her all the sins of living single. Life was fun then (except for cleaning and paying the bills) simple and uncomplicated.

In 1986, my brother Dave and I became roommates until his company transferred him to California. He'd met a woman from his work before they were transferred; they planned a Twin Cities June wedding in 1987, even though they were by then living in California. Kathy had been dating a wonderful man for a couple of years, and they planned to get married that October. My parents were sure glad I wasn't dating anyone seriously. I don't think they could've handled all three children getting married in one year.

During this time in my life, I'd become tired of the dating scene. Finding men in bars was out of the question as it seemed most of them were drunks or just wanted a one-night stand. The prospects of meeting someone at work were slim to none. I was working at a bank mortgage company at the time, and the few men working there were either spoken for or gay. I'd run out of friends with single guy acquaintances too.

As a joke, one of my friends from work brought in a magazine that was strictly personal ads called "Meet People." At first we had a good laugh, but after reading a few, I realized many of these people were like me. They were looking for a decent relationship and seemed sincere. I decided to answer a couple ads, then put in an ad for myself. I received a total of about 50 responses over the next several weeks. The majority seemed strange and I didn't dare answer them. The few I did answer provided me with a few nice dates, but nothing exciting.

One day, I glanced through the latest issue with my own ad and noticed one about a nice country guy who was a year younger than me, and lived in the town where I grew up. I decided to answer it, mostly because I wanted to know if I knew him. He called me and we talked for quite awhile. He told me he was building a house in White Bear Lake, but didn't grow up there so I hadn't previously known him. His house was nearing completion and it kept him very busy, so we weren't able to meet until November. Since my sister was getting married in October, I was busy too. We finally met at the Ground Round Restaurant on November 5, 1987.

I was instantly attracted to this man. The strange thing was, when he described the house he designed, it sounded remarkably like a house I had dreamed about a few years before, so he invited me over to see it a few days later, and it *was* strikingly similar to my dream. Kurt and I dated for a year when he asked me to marry him on Christmas. He was quite imaginative about the way he went about it. He hid pieces of paper all over the house, each one giving a clue to the next. I wasn't cooperating the way he would've liked, since I couldn't guess the clues, and he had to help me. When I finally found all the pieces of paper, I had to put them together like a jigsaw puzzle, which gave the final clue. This led me to a ceramic duck where the engagement ring was hidden. Not only is this guy romantic and sweet, but also mighty clever.

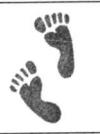 # Chapter Three

We were married on one of the hottest days that summer July 8, 1989. The ceremony was in a little church that held only 120 people. We had our reception outside, at Kurt's brother and sister-in-law's house, so I prayed months in advance for no rain. It did rain in the morning before the wedding, but cleared up and was *very hot* the rest of the day. Except for the heat, we had a picture perfect wedding, then a beautiful getaway afterward in western Wisconsin.

That house Kurt had built didn't fit our needs if we were to ever have children, so Kurt had sold it and designed a new one before our wedding. Because of government red tape, our new house wasn't quite finished by the time we were married, so we borrowed my parents' RV and lived in it the first week of our marriage.

I'll never forget that horrible first night. There was a swampy pond on the garage side of the house and as soon as the sun went down, the mosquitoes came out. There must've been a small opening somewhere in the RV because we were attacked by thousands of those pesky critters. We had to close all of the windows and vents in 90 degree weather and spend the rest of the night slapping bugs. To this day the thought of that nonstop buzzing makes me shiver. The next evening wasn't quite as bad, since we invested in Raid and lots of mosquito repellent.

The next week we went to a lake up north for our honeymoon. Though it was a small mobile home, it seemed like a castle compared to what we'd been living in. We had a lot of fun, and when we got back, our new house had electricity and running water so we could finally move in. Even though it was just a shell without sheetrocked walls and bare wood floors, it was still better than the RV.

I became a very creative cook since we didn't have a kitchen. We borrowed my parents' portable electric hot plate used for camping and had a microwave on a table, a new refrigerator, and a gas grill. It's amazing the meals you can cook on a gas grill, even a frozen pizza. The only sink we had at the time was in the laundry room and there were no cupboards either. Our dishes were in boxes, so we used paper plates most of the time. It was like camping out in our own home.

We worked on the house every day after work and went to bed thoroughly exhausted. One evening just before we fell asleep, Kurt sat up and said, "Isn't that cricket driving you crazy?" I couldn't understand how one little cricket in the house could keep him awake.

I told him to forget it, but he ended up walking around the house in the middle of the night in his underwear, with a can of Raid, until all was quiet again.

It took about a year to complete that house. It eventually

became quite beautiful, like something right out of *Better Homes and Gardens* magazine. It had a hand-made spiral staircase in the master suite which Kurt made from a large oak tree. This extended up to an octagonal room surrounded with windows and a deck over the double garage. There was also a sitting room off the master bedroom with a balcony you could look over to view the kitchen and dining room area. Unfortunately, this gorgeous place required two full-time incomes, and I wanted to work only part-time after we had children. This decision led us to sell that house too, and design still another. This time I insisted on a finished interior with a complete kitchen before we'd move in.

House number three was totally different than the last one. It was rustic and set way back in the woods. We had quite a few problems in getting the house built due to excessive rain and clay soil. Our road, nicknamed driveway from hell, was a block and a half long, and had to be totally redesigned, which brought the excavating cost to over $10,000.00. Everyone got stuck in that driveway. The person who delivered the roof trusses didn't even bother putting them near the house. In order to avoid all the mud, he dropped the huge trusses at the top of the driveway and hurried on his way. Lucky for us, the excavator was a great guy who helped us over and above what we paid him to do. He moved the trusses for us and pulled out numerous construction vehicles, including his own.

During the construction we had to rent a place for a few months. We'd informed the landlord when the house was scheduled to be finished so they could locate another tenant. Unfortunately the house didn't go as planned, and they had found another tenant before we were ready to move, so my lovely sister and brother-in-law let us stay in their basement for the next month or so.

This happened in August 1991, and I was already four months pregnant. Except for the morning sickness and a few headaches in my first trimester, I felt pretty good. Being pregnant for the first time was real fun for me. I got a lot of attention at work since I was one of the first in a group of women to get pregnant.

We moved into our home in September, unpacked, and were settled right before the Halloween blizzard which hit the Twin Cities area in 1991. Poor Kurt spent the whole next day snowplowing driveway from hell over and over again.

Around Thanksgiving, Kurt's father fell ill and was diagnosed with lung cancer. The doctor told him it was a slow growing cancer but this type is usually not discovered until it has become well established, so they started chemotherapy and radiation right away. He didn't feel well by Christmas time, but had a good attitude and kept in good spirits.

He was always the type of person that saw good in everything and everybody. It was a good Christmas that year—actually, the last stress-free Christmas that I can remember.

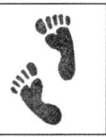

Chapter Four

Then our first child was born on January 23, 1992 everyone was thrilled. We named him Jesse Fritz (his middle name given after both grandfathers). The next youngest grandchild on both sides of the family was already 13 years old, so they were ready to spoil our new son.

Jesse was an active infant; Kurt and I had a hard time feeding him. He'd flare his little arms and knock the bottle out of his mouth, then get upset because he was hungry. We found by putting his arms down by his sides, wrapping him tight in his blanket, we could feed him easily and he'd fall asleep. My mother-in-law thought this approach was awful.

"He looks like a little mummy all wrapped up like that!" she exclaimed.

I assured her that he liked it and could wriggle free after he was put in his crib.

Unfortunately, when he got older it was harder for him to fall asleep without first being wrapped up. We also noticed that certain noises bothered him too. Whenever anyone sniffed or blew a nose, Jesse would cry like he was in pain. During the summer when Kurt used the chainsaw to clean up all the dead trees around the yard I had to shut all the windows, bring Jesse to the opposite end of the house and cover his ears, but he could still hear the wailing of the saw and cried. Since he was our first child and we had no one to compare him to, he seemed to progress the same as any other child under a year old. We thought maybe he was just a little more sensitive than other children.

Chapter Five

Kurt's father became extremely ill with his cancer by June, 1992. Kurt, his three brothers and two sisters were able to take turns helping their mother with their father. Kurt's sister and brother-in-law had medical degrees, so they were able to keep track of all the medicines he had to take. This poor man was in so much pain, but just didn't want to leave his wife of 49 years. "I really wanted to make it to our 50th year anniversary" he told her.

When the rest of the family was in the living room we could hear him on the monitor asking his wife if she was going to be okay. He was always more concerned about her than about his own problem. They had such a wonderful marriage, it made me sick to think they would soon be separated.

In July, Dad became so incapacitated that everyone took turns staying overnight. The night Kurt, Jesse and I were there, he'd have to sit up in bed in order to breathe better. He just kept staring at the wall. I asked him what he was looking at. He was quite groggy from all the drugs and hard to understand, but informed us there was a hole in the wall.

We tried to see what he was looking at, but only found a small nail hole. He seemed irritated that we weren't seeing it, and I silently wondered if he was viewing the other side of existence. I'd read a few books and knew of a couple people personally who'd had near death experiences, so I thought maybe he could see that tunnel with the bright light at the end of it. It still remains a mystery to this day.

We stayed with them Saturday night through Sunday morning, and I laid in bed all night wondering if he'd die while we were there. I didn't know what to do, or even know if I'd be any help, so I prayed for strength to be given to all of us.

Since I didn't work on Monday, I wouldn't stop at Kurt's parents' house, even though all day something kept nagging me to go see Dad. It was a 30 mile drive from our house to theirs so I decided against it and figured Kurt would stop by on his way home anyway. I noticed it was fairly early when Kurt got home, so I asked if he stopped in to see his dad. To my disappointment he hadn't, so I tried to tell myself I'd see him tomorrow after work, but my guts told me different.

It was a little after 10:00 p.m. when we got to bed and Kurt received the call from his brother. I remember Kurt's face when he got the call. He didn't need to say a thing with that awful look on his face. We immediately got dressed, put sleeping Jesse in his car seat and drove out to be with his family.

When we arrived, his family was there paying their last respects and supporting their mother. Kurt's mom was still in the bedroom with Dad's body, and when we walked in I felt the most incredible love and overwhelming peace in that room. I thought I'd be upset seeing that man's body lying there, but wasn't at all. The love was so strong I didn't even want to leave. Kurt took a seat near the door with six month old Jesse on his lap, when suddenly Jesse looked directly above where grandpa was lying and giggled. It was exactly like when grandpa used to play with Jesse's feet and say "One two, one two." We all stopped and stared at the boy. Finally grandma said, "Do you think grandpa is saying good-bye?"

The love and warmth stayed in that house for over a week. Kurt liked going over there even though his dad was gone, because of how he felt when he'd walk in the house.

Kurt, Jesse, our dog Sheeba and I went to a cabin for a week with his family a little over a week after the funeral. It just wasn't the same without Dad. One evening after Jesse and Kurt went to bed, I stayed up late with his sister Janie and their aunt. We sat by the lake talking about her father, when we heard a big splash. The lake was totally calm except for the ripples from the splash. The three of us smiled and Janie said "Must be Dad catching the big one!"

When we got back from the cabin, Kurt noticed the feeling in his mother's house was gone. Thanksgiving and Christmas weren't the same usual joyous occasions. Not only was it sad, but it was hard on Jesse. He couldn't handle loud noises and crowds very well, and with two more children recently born into that family, the noise level was even louder than usual.

Missing Kurt's father, I cried a lot during that time but not Kurt. I couldn't understand why he didn't cry. He told me he knew his dad was in a better place, no longer in pain, and his death was expected. Of course I knew all that, but the fact was he was gone and I missed him!

 # Chapter Six

In January, my girlfriend Barb, who lived in Texas, called and gave me some exciting news. She and her boyfriend were going to get married in October. She told me not to tell anyone in her family, since they were coming home the first of March for her cousin's wedding and wanted to tell everyone the good news all at once.

I was so excited for her; she had been through some bad relationships in the past. Every time I received a depressing letter from her, I prayed for her guidance to find a decent man. Once she met Mark, she didn't have much time to write, but when she did, the letters were always upbeat and positive. She finally seemed happy, and I was looking forward to meeting this man.

Barb and Mark were invited over for dinner on March 3rd, and I was disappointed when they arrived late. They apologized, saying they were at the Mall of America and it took a lot longer than they expected. We had a nice dinner, and Barb was grateful Jesse was so quiet and passive while we were eating. She was tired of all the excessive chatter from her nieces and nephews during the week. After dinner Kurt took Jesse and went in the living room with Mark. Barb and I were cleaning the kitchen when she asked me what I thought of him. I said she picked a winner, and I guess we both had to kiss a few frogs before we got our prince!

We had a nice, but short talk since I had to put Jesse to bed. I tried wrapping him up as usual and giving him a bottle in the living room, but there was too much activity going on for him to settle down. I brought him in our bedroom and became angry at myself for not allowing him to put himself to sleep when he was an infant. Now at 13 months old I was still holding him until he'd fall asleep, then carefully put him in his crib so he wouldn't wake up.

When I finally joined them, Barb said they had to leave soon because she was getting a cold and wanted to get to bed early. I was sad their visit was so short, and told them they couldn't leave until I took their picture. Barb always hated people taking her picture, and this was no exception. She said I could take as many pictures as I wanted on their wedding day, so I gave in and she took a picture of us instead.

By the end of March we were in the planning stages of selling our house again. We found two pieces of property side-by-side so Kurt's brother could build next door. This fourth house would enable me to completely quit my job, so I was willing to sacrifice my sanity one more time.

On Saturday, March 20, 1993 Kurt and another carpenter were finishing the basement when the phone rang. I was putting Jesse in his crib for a nap, so Kurt answered it.

It was Barb's brother. When I got to the phone, he blurted out, "Barb died this morning." This guy was the joker of their family, so I thought this must be some sort of sick joke. Then I heard his voice begin to shake and suddenly knew this was no joke. He proceeded to tell me that when they returned to Texas, Barb's cold got worse. She stayed home from work for a few days, which wasn't like her. When her girlfriend called, Barb sounded so out of it she had Mark go check on her. Mark immediately brought her to the hospital, and after running tests, they found she was diabetic and had her stay in the hospital a week, for observation.

The nurse came in early Saturday morning to ask how she felt, and Barb said, "Good. They're going to release me today." The nurse told her she'd be back in 15 minutes before her shift was over, to make sure Barb knew how to take her insulin. When the nurse came back, Barb was dead! They think she died due to a blood clot, but they'll find out more with an autopsy.

So many thoughts raced through my head as he was telling me this. First I thought this was all just a dream and I'm going to wake up any minute. I wondered why Barb? She's too young! I so wished I'd insisted on taking their picture, because I wanted to see her face once more. When I got off the phone, I went to Kurt shaking uncontrollably and barely able to speak. When I finally did get words out, he could barely understand them through my sobs.

Barb's family brought her body back here for the funeral and burial by the end of the week. I'd hoped to be in control of myself by then, but when I walked in the funeral home and saw her in the casket then looked at Mark, I hugged him and started to cry all over again.

I had a very difficult time with Barb's death. She was only 33 years old and her life was just beginning. It didn't make sense. My biggest concern was for Barb herself. Was she really at peace now? Was she upset about having to leave Mark? Had her time spent on earth really been completed? I prayed daily for understanding to these questions and to be granted inner peace.

One afternoon I was lying on my bed feeding Jesse a bottle before his nap. He was wide awake and I wondered if he was going to fight sleep like he sometimes did. I laid there admiring him, when I noticed his gaze.

His eyes were looking up towards the ceiling and moving back and forth as if watching a conversation. Then I suddenly felt this wonderful warmth throughout my body, from head to toe. It enveloped me so completely that my usually cold hands and feet were comfortably warm. I shut my eyes and received that same incredible love I felt after Kurt's dad had died, only this time it was even stronger. I knew it was Barb's presence with me and I finally felt at peace with her death. The feelings this experience gave me let me know she was in a marvelous place with total serenity. All of this happened in less than a minute and when I opened my eyes, I felt tears of joy streaming down my face. I looked down at Jesse who'd been awake only seconds earlier. He was now fast asleep.

I can't explain what happened, I only know that my deep sadness for Barb was taken away, and I hoped and prayed that Mark and her family received the same inner peace that I got. Selfishly I still miss her, but I know she's really the lucky one to be in that better place.

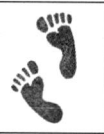 # Chapter Seven

We sold our house before it had a chance to be put on the market, so we started another house immediately. In order to save money and help out my sister and brother-in-law at the same time, again we stayed in their basement and paid them rent while building the house. We had a separate entrance and kitchen so it was a nice temporary place to stay. Kurt also helped Darrell fix a few things around their house with his free time, giving an added benefit to having us as renters. We gave Jesse the bedroom and put our bed in the living room. All of our furniture was in storage, so the bed was also used as a couch. As our new house was nearing completion, and we were getting ready to move in, I found out I was pregnant.

We were all excited since the pregnancy was planned, except for my poor niece Heather, who was grossed out when she realized I had gotten pregnant in their house! All-in-all I liked that time living close to Kathy, even though it was a little too cozy.

When it was time for us three to move into our new house, Kathy and I were in tears. We loved being neighbors, and the thought of being 25 minutes away compared to two seconds away was hard on both of us.

Emotionally, I became a basket case. My job was stressing me out and we still had a lot of things to finish on the house. I couldn't understand why I wasn't happy with this pregnancy. Nothing was physically wrong with me or the baby, but my gut feelings told me something was not right. I tried to rationalize my feelings, and tell myself most women worry about their unborn babies.

Before I knew it, it was Thanksgiving and I decided to quit my job at the end of the year to be a stay home mom. I hoped leaving this job would alleviate some of my emotional stress which it did, but only slightly. For Kurt this baby couldn't come soon enough. Not only was he tired of a crabby wife, but was also quite sick of macaroni and cheese, which I constantly craved.

When I left my job, instead of rolling over the retirement funds that had accumulated, we finished the floors, bought window coverings, and purchased a hot tub. I was upset that I couldn't use the hot tub since I was pregnant, but it came in handy that summer because we turned down the heat, and I used it to cool off on those awful hot days.

Kurt's brother Marty, and his wife Robin built their house next door to us, and because everyone had a minimum of five acres, the neighborhood was spread out. The families near our home were all terrific and made us feel welcome as soon as we moved in.

One afternoon, one of our neighbors Chris, and I were sitting at the dining room table chatting. I was telling her my concern with Jesse not talking and figured by age two and a half he should be saying more than just mama and daddy. She said she wouldn't be too concerned, since Einstein didn't even talk until he was four. Just then, Jesse ran past us into the kitchen and said "Oreo." We both laughed, and I said, "Oh sure, he knows the most important word in a kid's life!"

Our second son, Clint Matthew, was born June 25, 1994. He had beautiful big blue eyes, a little tiny nose and cute chubby cheeks. He seemed so perfect, and I told myself, see—you had nothing to worry about. The day after we took Clint home from the hospital, he slept all night. I woke up early that morning in a panic, ran in to check on him, and found him sleeping soundly. Ever since one of the women at work lost her eight month old daughter to SIDS, it became one of my worst fears.

The next day, my mother stopped over to help me with Jesse and some chores, when she commented on how noisy and choking Clint seemed when he drank from his bottle and how he'd arch his back. She'd seen many babies, but none who did that. I didn't pay much attention, since he seemed fine to me.

A few weeks later, mom went to Iowa to help my cousin Janet, and her husband Duane. Duane was dying of cancer and wanted to die at home like Kurt's father. My heart and prayers went out to them, as the memory of Kurt's dad was still fresh in my mind. It's nice to have the chance to be able to say good-bye to a loved one, but watching the pain they endure without being able to help them is awful. Janet understood why I couldn't make it to the funeral after Duane died on August 8, 1994, since Clint was so young. I felt bad even though I knew her house would be full of relatives and I probably wouldn't be missed.

Mom was physically and mentally exhausted when she came home, and I felt guilty asking her to watch the boys so I could help my mother-in-law with her garage sale. Thankfully, my mother was quick to get back to normal living and looked forward to seeing Jesse and Clint.

On opening day at the garage sale, a woman came in with her baby who looked to be about Clint's age. I noticed the baby was holding her head up on her own, so I asked how old she was. The mother said she was ten weeks old, so I figured Clint, being eight weeks, still had a couple weeks to go before he'd be doing that. Another week went by, but Clint was still not holding his head up.

My instincts were telling me something wasn't right, so I decided to watch videos of Jesse and noticed he held his head up just fine at Clint's age. I was concerned, but talked myself into not comparing Clint with other children, since they all progress at different rates.

"My life is good!" I said to Kurt while sitting in the hot tub one cool evening in September. "I have a fabulous house, a wonderful husband, two beautiful boys and a sweet good natured dog, what more could a person hope for?" Even with all this, I silently wondered what my purpose here on earth was. Was I supposed to be doing something more productive? I had started a bookkeeping consultant business before Clint was born, but I felt I should be doing more, as if something was missing.

 # Chapter Eight

On Wednesday September 14, 1994, I was changing Clint's diaper, when all of a sudden his eyes opened wide, his face tensed, and his lips turned blue. It looked as though he was choking and my first thought was, "Omigod!—a SIDS baby. I've caught an apnea episode. I panicked—I didn't know infant CPR. Grabbing him from the changing table, I blew in his face to see if he'd breathe in. He didn't respond. I ran downstairs with him to call 911, but when I got to the bottom of the stairs, he began acting normal again. I was shaking so hard, I could barely punch in the pediatrician's number. They advised me to take him to Children's Hospital in St. Paul immediately. I quickly called my mom to watch Jesse, then paged Kurt at work. We met at his mother's so we could ride together to the hospital. After telling Kurt the whole story, we rode in silence.

It took over an hour before we were able to see a doctor in the ER. When she came in, I explained to her how he behaved at home, and when she finished examining him, she turned to me and started asking questions. I wondered if this doctor thought I was crazy, because Clint looked and acted just fine. Had I really only imagined this? For a brief moment I doubted my own sanity.

Just then Clint tensed up. I pointed at him and exclaimed, "Look! He's doing it again!" Thank God I'm not crazy, I reasoned.

The doctor calmly said she wanted one of their neurologists to look at him, so we sat and waited another hour before he came in. He asked the same questions and performed a similar exam when Clint had another episode. The neurologist put oxygen on him, and said he wanted to have an MRI done, which they scheduled immediately. We went straight over to that area, but had to wait another hour before they brought him in. He had a fourth episode when the nurse was ready to bring him into the room and she wasn't as calm as the doctors had been. She scrambled for the oxygen, and when I saw how she reacted, my stomach did flip flops. It suddenly dawned on me he was doing this every hour and a half, and I mentioned this to the nurse.

Kurt noticed quite a few doctors going into the room during Clint's MRI. When the doctor came out, he said he wanted to keep Clint overnight for an EEG and observation. They admitted him to a room and started to superglue electrodes to his head while advising us to go home and get some rest. Part of me longed to stay with my baby, but the doctors wanted him sound asleep for their EEG.

We'd been at the hospital for over 10 hours and Kurt thought it'd be wise for us to eat and get some rest, so I arranged to have my mother keep Jesse overnight. I wanted to be back in the hospital first thing in the morning. We didn't eat much, and we tossed and turned all night. I lay there trying to reassure myself that whatever is wrong with our child, the doctors would be able to fix it.

The next morning I went straight to the hospital but Kurt decided to go to work. His job site was close to the hospital that day, so I'd page him when I knew more about Clint's condition. The doctor was busy doing his rounds when I arrived, so I had to wait. The intern came by and asked me if Kurt would be arriving soon but I told her he had to work.

When the doctor arrived he immediately inquired about my husband. My response was, "If he doesn't work he doesn't get paid," his reaction was to look down at the floor, pause, and say, "Well, I was hoping I could have you both here." The look on his face and tone of his voice gave me a sharp tug in my stomach. "Clint has a rare brain disorder called lissencephaly." Slowly he continued, "Lissencephaly comes from two words, *lissen*—meaning smooth—and *cephaly*—meaning brain, both of which mean that kids with this disease don't develop the bumps and grooves on their brains as they develop. They're mentally handicapped anywhere from moderate to severe."

I went completely numb, but something sensible inside me knew I wouldn't stay that way for long. The only thing I could think of was paging Kurt. I needed my husband NOW. When he returned the page, he wanted the information over the phone. When I started stammering a few words, it left poor Kurt all confused and angry. He couldn't understand why I couldn't give him the complete information over the phone, and I said he obviously needed to hear the doctor explain it better.

While we waited for Kurt to arrive, the neurologist told me more about our baby's condition. He said these children develop hard-to-control seizures and usually won't outlive their parents. Immediately I wanted to know everything we'd have to deal with. He said he wasn't an expert on lissencephaly, but he did know of a man at the University of Minnesota named Dr. William Dobyns who was. I needed to read any information they had about this disease, and the intern said she would make copies of whatever she could find and get them to me. When the doctor left for a few minutes, I said to the intern, "My biggest fear used to be having a SIDS baby, now I really don't know what's worse!" Tears suddenly filled her eyes, and she put her arm around me. That's when I finally lost my composure and sobbed.

Kurt walked into Clint's room about a half an hour after I had paged him, but to me it seemed like hours. The neurologist filled him in on what he'd already told me. My stomach was so upset I felt as if I was going to be sick. All I could do was stare at my beautiful, perfect-looking little boy in that crib. It was hard for me to believe anything could be wrong with him. My faith in God was strong, but as I looked at my son, I wondered if this was some sort of test.

The neurologist needed to keep Clint in the hospital for still another day so they could start him on the seizure medication phenobarbital, then they gave me a few numbers of people I could call. One of them was Dr. Dobyns, a pediatric neurologist who specialized in lissencephaly, and the other was a woman who began the Lissencephaly Support Network. The doctor and intern advised us to contact our school district and county offices for information on financial aid for children with disabilities.

That night at home, I read everything the intern gave me, (which really wasn't much and mostly written in medical jargon). Shock set in the next day and I don't even remember bringing Clint home from the hospital. I called a good friend from my old job who had a Down syndrome girl. I remembered one of our conversations about her doctor telling her to have her baby institutionalized after she was born but thankfully she didn't listen to those doctors. I made a few sobbing phone calls to her because I knew she'd understand, but as I look back on it now I wish I hadn't. She was struggling with breast cancer at the time, and obviously had her own problems to deal with. The problem was, she was the only one I knew who had a child with a disability.

I called to make an appointment with Dr. Dobyns right away, but was told they couldn't get us in for at least a month. I needed more questions answered, so I called Dianna of the Lissencephaly Network. It was nice to talk to someone who'd already been through similar circumstances. When I told her we were going to see Dr. Dobyns, she said we were lucky to be in that area. People from all over the world come to see him. Unfortunately, most of the people are hoping he can fix their children. He's a wealth of knowledge, but sadly there's no cure. Dianna sent me a packet of information, which I gratefully received before the end of the week.

I called the school district next, and they met with Clint and me on October 13, 1994. At the end of the meeting, one of the teachers asked if we had any questions about our older son Jesse and I replied, "As a matter of fact, I do—he's over two and a half and still not talking. People tell me not to compare my child with others, but I think he should be at least *trying* to speak." The teachers agreed and we set up another appointment to evaluate Jesse.

The whole month of October becomes a blur to me now after Jesse was determined "delayed in speech and fine motor skills." I do remember thinking "delayed" seemed like no big deal compared to Clint, who wouldn't mentally grow beyond the age of about three months, but I did realize at this point that I'd need a support group for myself. I found one right away meeting on Monday afternoons, and those women were wonderful. I instantly felt at ease and comfortable enough to open up to all of them.

As we introduced ourselves, I learned I wouldn't be the only one with two handicapped children; the majority of them had boys with autism. I listened closely to them when they discussed their kids and many of their sons' mannerisms were exactly the same as Jesse's. On my drive home, I thought of the boys Evey took care of 18 years ago at the group home and wondered, could Jesse be autistic too?

 # Chapter Nine

Since Jesse and Clint were still under three years old, their teachers came to our house. Both had the same teacher and occupational therapist, but Jesse also had a speech therapist. They usually came at the same time so there wouldn't be someone coming over every day. I asked one of their teachers if she thought Jesse was autistic. She couldn't say one way or another, since she wasn't an expert, but she did give me one of her books to read. It was written by a woman named Temple Grandin, who was autistic, and titled *Emergence.* I became anxious while reading it, since there were quite a few traits in Jesse that paralleled Temple's. I felt good about some of the things we did to Jesse when he was an infant. Temple emphasized the importance of stimulation from hugging and socializing. When we wrapped Jesse tight in his blanket as a baby, I learned it had helped him in the area of his sensory defensiveness. By getting him early childhood education, we were helping to pull him out of his own world.

With all the reading I did, teacher visits, county service people visits, going to doctors' appointments and attending the support group, I actually found time to do the state and county's paper work for Clint's medical services. I became so busy, I barely had time to grieve. Those few days I did have with my boys alone I spent crying. Holding Clint for hours, I'd sing "You Are My Special Angel," as tears poured out and splashed on his chubby little cheeks. Knowing I couldn't handle this alone, I talked to God daily.

Some days were so overwhelming I felt I couldn't even breathe. There were days when I needed a shoulder to cry on, and my poor mother got the brunt of my sobbing episodes. One day when I called her, I was so hysterical she thought someone got hurt or Clint had died. There were other days when morbid humor got us through difficult situations. If we didn't find something to laugh about, we'd cry. So laughter was the best therapy for us.

On October 27th, Kurt, Clint and I finally met the renowned expert, Dr. Dobyns. Since he worked at the university, we had to go through interns first before we could even speak to him. We spent all that afternoon sitting and waiting. When we finally saw the doctor, the three of us were tired and crabby, but I was prepared with a bunch of questions the poor man didn't even have answers for, such as when and how would our son die? He explained that since they continually aspirate their milk and food, most of these kids die from pneumonia, and who knows when that would be? Each cold they get weakens their systems more and more until eventually their bodies simply give out.

Dr. Dobyns diagnosed Clint with Miller-Dieker Syndrome Lissencephaly, which is considered one of the most severe forms, and many babies don't make it to their fifth birthday. Kurt and I had already decided there would be no heroic lifesaving procedures done for Clint. Dr. Dobyns understood this decision since he'd seen how these children live. However, he also assured us if we ever change our minds that would be okay too.

Later we had genetic blood tests done on the three of us to determine whether Clint's syndrome was a fluke of nature or a genetic problem on one of the parents' side. While waiting for the results (which took a minimum of six weeks) we considered our other options. We felt Jesse needed a sibling to grow up with, so we talked about adoption. If either of us had the genetic defect, it would've been too risky to conceive another child.

I'd take Clint to the University of Minnesota only for treatment of his seizures, but I really dreaded those days. Just getting there was always such a big production. Dropping Jesse off at my moms, driving, parking, getting Clint into his stroller, then maneuvering through elevators and tunnels would take us well over an hour and a half. The worst part of the appointment was getting his blood drawn, after we saw Dr. Dobyns. We had to make sure his seizure medication levels weren't too high, otherwise it could be toxic on his system. Poor Baby Clint's veins were so small, that only one person in the lab could find it, and when he wasn't there I felt like I was bringing him to a torture chamber. They'd wrap him up in this papoose thing with only his arm sticking out. If they didn't find the vein in one arm, they'd try the other, the whole time Clint would be screaming!

On his regular baby check ups, he went to Jesse's pediatrician which was near our home. Those doctors had never heard of lissencephaly before, so I had to supply copies of all my reading material. Then everyone in the clinic would know what to expect of Clint.

The first few months it was so hard to believe anything was wrong with him since he looked so normal. As he grew, however, you could tell something was different since he couldn't hold his head up, but to people passing by, he just looked like a tired boy in a stroller.

By the end of October, Robin and Marty announced they were going to have a second child. Robin found out she was pregnant the same day Clint was diagnosed, but didn't think it was a good time to tell us then, figuring we wouldn't take the news very enthusiastically. I was so thrilled with their news that Robin was surprised by my reaction. It would've been nice to have heard something wonderful and positive last month, but I understood why they waited.

I always loved Halloween, but this year I just wasn't in the spirit. The best I could do was dress Jesse up as his favorite stuffed animal Tigger. Since Clint looked like Baby Simba, we didn't think he even needed an outfit.

November settled down a bit, and I started a journal which helped me deal with all my runaway emotions. On November 6th, we met a couple who'd had a child with Clint's diagnosis and their son had died in 1989. The mother was a pediatrician at the health clinic where I used to take Jesse when I was still working. Jesse's former pediatrician was also their son's pediatrician, so he probably would've recognized Clint's condition immediately. This made me wonder about God's plan again—did Clint's current doctors need to learn from Clint?

I think getting together with this couple helped us all. They were interested in seeing another child with Miller-

Which one's Simba?

Halloween 1994

Dieker Syndrome, and told us what to expect when he gets sick, since they didn't do any heroic lifesaving procedures with their son either.

I don't know if all my rationalizing was part of the grieving process or not, but I desperately needed to know that Clint's life here was not just a waste. I tried justifying why he was put here on this earth and in *our* family. I wanted to think maybe he was here for us to learn from him. I was angry that we couldn't *fix* our son, so I prayed a lot for peace and understanding.

Bedtime was a lengthy and tiresome process at our house. Kurt and I would first put Jesse to bed since he was easier. Next came Clint, and I began an involved ritual. First I'd get him ready for bed of course, with diaper, pajamas and wrapped in his blanket. Then came crushing up his phenobarbital until it became a powder, adding formula so it could be sucked up in a syringe. Then, while holding Clint, I'd have to squeeze the syringe into the side of his mouth to make it easier for him to swallow. This was followed with a regular bottle to help him to wash it all down. But sucking on a nipple wasn't easy for him. The older he got, the more he inhaled part of his milk. Some nights, this routine could take up to an hour and half.

This took so long, I got into the habit of watching TV until he'd fall asleep in my arms. Kurt got terribly frustrated when I did this, since he wanted time alone with me. I explained to him that since we'd be together a lot longer than with Clint, I wanted to hold him as much as I could.

Kurt and I dealt with our grief so differently. I wanted to spend as much time as I could with Clint and tried to memorize everything about him, while Kurt wanted the opposite. He needed to put distance between himself and the boy so he wouldn't miss him so much when he died. It was as if Clint was becoming only my boy and Jesse was Kurt's. At first I became angry with him. I couldn't understand why he didn't feel the same way I did.

As time went by, I never did totally understand, but I grew to accept and respect his feelings; I guess everyone has to grieve differently and at different times.

I decided it would be a good idea to have a family photo taken to send to our friends in their Christmas cards, so Kurt's brother Marty took the pictures at our house in November.

Kurt, Me, Jesse, Clint & Sheeba November '94

December and January were not good months. The only way to explain the beginning of December is by my journal, which reads:

Monday, December 12, 1994

In a matter of one and a half hours, I turned into a screaming idiot! Kurt went to the neighbors to check out what kind of computer we should buy, and within minutes after he left, Clint started screaming like a raving lunatic. I couldn't do anything to calm him down. He wouldn't take milk, water, his nuk, he didn't want me to cuddle him, and he screamed even louder when I put him down. I tried to change him and he peed all over his p.j.'s and blanket. By this time I'm a raving lunatic too. I'm screaming and stomping around. Sheeba gets all nervous and gets in my way no matter where I go. I'm trying to get upstairs to get another blanket out of Jesse's room and Sheeba's standing in my way. I say "MOVE" and she runs in our bedroom with her tail between her legs. By the time Kurt gets home, everything is settled down...of course.

I noticed after that insane evening, Clint started having new seizures called infantile spasms. These seizures can do additional brain damage if they're not controlled and sometimes babies can lose any ability they have, including sucking. I'm sure that's why he was so irritable, but I don't know if it would've helped *me* that night.

Dr. Dobyns suggested we try putting him on a drug called ACTH which might possibly have a chance of curing the seizures so he'd never need daily medication. I've since labeled this medicine drug from hell.

First, it required Clint be in the hospital under observation for three days, making sure his blood pressure didn't get too high from it. They warned me he'd swell up and become extremely hungry, but who could imagine it would get as bad as it did? The hospital personnel trained me to give him an injection every morning in first one, then the other of his chubby little thighs. I felt like a horrible mom inflicting pain on him like this, especially when we eventually found that the seizures didn't diminish as expected.

For two months this went on, with Clint slowly swelling up so badly his entire body resembled a nine-months-pregnant belly—a face so puffy he had slits for eyes instead of his usual large Bambi eyes. He was stiff, cranky, and ravenously hungry.

He drank an 8-oz. bottle every three hours, so every 24-hour period he ingested a gallon of formula, and I became a zombie, since I had to get up and feed him every few hours.

Christmas was an awful time for Clint. Even though I warned everyone that his skin was very sensitive and he'd rather be left alone, they still passed him around from one relative to another. His unrelenting cries disturbed me so badly, that I finally took him away from everyone, brought him to his room, fed him a bottle where it was nice and quiet, then put him to bed.

At our appointment in January, the intern suggested we up the dosage. Well, I almost lost it! I did manage to maintain my composure long enough to say firmly, "I wanted him taken off this NOW. Our main goal is to keep

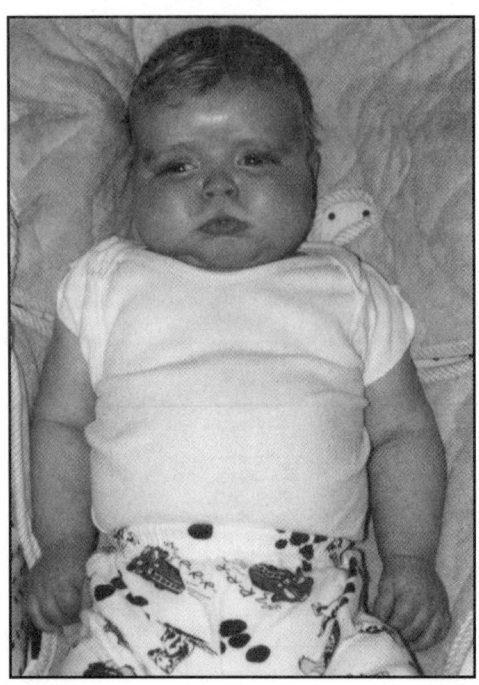

Clint as comfortable as possible in his short little life, and ACTH certainly is not doing that!" Thank the Lord Dr. Dobyns agreed and quietly informed the intern that it doesn't always work on some kids. He suggested we start him on another drug called depakene instead.

The awful part was weaning Clint slowly off ACTH. He couldn't be free of it until the end of the month. The week after we started him on phenobarbital and depakene his seizures decreased. It made me sick to think we put him through that misery for nothing. It seems scary that people with seizures can be only helpless guinea pigs for all these seizure medications.

 # Chapter Ten

Kurt and I got good news in January about our genetic blood tests. Neither of us was a carrier of a bad gene; the chances of us having another child like Clint was only 0.1%. We decided we'd have another right away, so the new baby and Jesse wouldn't be too far apart in age. I prayed a lot over this one, asking God to show me if this was the right thing for us to do. I believed if it wasn't meant to be, I wouldn't get pregnant right away.

At the end of January, when Jesse had his 3-year check up, he was given a different doctor; within five minutes of checking him over she suspected he was autistic and gave me the number of a specialist. Of course I called right away to make the appointment but wasn't able to get him in until March 16th.

Jesse got the flu with vomiting and diarrhea in February. It was so bad, but the doctors said they usually don't do anything until it's been at least 3-4 weeks. At one point he was becoming dehydrated, so we brought him to the emergency room on a Friday. Jesse fought being touched, with the little strength he had left, and the doctor said he wasn't dehydrated since he had enough energy to fight him off.

On Monday I brought him to the pediatricians and they found he had a major ear infection. When he started recovering from the flu, he got a cough and runny nose, then I got the bug. He ended up taking three different antibiotics for his ear infection, which gave him diarrhea all over again! Clint came down with the same cold, which settled into his lungs. He did manage to fight it off, but Dr. Dobyns reminded me it could get harder for him next time. At that time we decided to ask Dr. Dobyns write up a DNR letter (Do Not Resuscitate), which we kept with Clint at all times.

I usually wrote in my journal whenever there were many things I had to deal with all at once, and March was one of them. These are my notes taken directly from that journal:

Friday March 17, 1995

It's 6:30 a.m. and I just finished feeding Clint. He seems to aspirate his milk an awful lot now. Sometimes I think we're not going to have him here much longer. I just can't bear thinking I won't be able to kiss his face all the time. I talked to a woman who lives in Washington who had a boy with Miller-Dieker Syndrome and died when he was 2 1/2. She said she never felt she could let her son go, until the week before her son's death, and then she finally felt at peace with it. I've always accepted Clint's death, because I know he'll be in a better place, but I can't help my selfish feelings. I will always want to kiss the top of his little head and say how much I love him! He has such a sweet disposition, that it's hard to say good-bye to that lovely little soul. I know he'll be waiting for me when I go to the other side, and I'll be able to kiss and hug him again. It's just going to be hard to wait. I'll have so many others to see up in heaven too! I'm sobbing while writing this. I'm sure my hormones are kicking in, since I just found out Monday I'm pregnant! I'm due November 5, 1995. The date Kurt and I met 8 years ago.

Yesterday Jesse and I went to see the autism specialist and she diagnosed him with autism. She feels he's extremely high functioning and will have no problem in school, but we need to do extra work with him, such as a personal care attendant. She made me feel real good, by saying we did everything right, and I'm very good to him. It's now 7:00 a.m. and I hear Jesse getting restless. I can hardly wait until daylight savings time, since Jesse gets up with the sun, just like his father!

Tuesday March 28, 1995

It's 7:30 p.m. and I just put Clint to bed. He's been screaming since 5:30. Luckily we ate early. One of Kurt's friends from work wanted to look at our scuba equipment we're selling. On his way over here, he hit a deer. Kurt and he are back by the deer right now waiting for the police. It's been an awful night for everyone so far. Jesse fell off his shelf and bruised his back and shin right before Kurt's friend came in with the bad news.

Nights like this I, wonder why we decided to have another child. We think it's bad having to put two to bed, what about three!

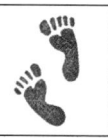# Chapter Eleven

Since November, people had been coming to our house almost every day. I kept a calendar by the phone in the kitchen, just to keep track of daily events. Every morning while preparing Clint's medicine, I'd check the calendar to see what was happening that day. If it didn't get written down I wouldn't remember, as forgetting things seemed to happen a lot. I didn't know whether to blame it on my pregnancy, depression, or that I was just too damn busy all the time!

May was an interesting month, as one of my girlfriends, T.J. and her fiancee came here from Colorado to get married on May 5th. One of our mutual friends, her husband and their two children came up from Louisiana for the wedding and stayed with Kurt and me for close to a week. I thought it'd be too stressful having a housefull, but surprisingly it was the opposite. It was fun having them here. They made themselves at home, helped make meals, and cleaned up too.

During the weekend of the wedding, I got poison oak and it spread to parts of my face. By Sunday the right side of my face was so swollen that I went to the hospital near my home. I was nervous about it with pregnancy and felt better having it checked out.

The doctor assured me it wouldn't affect the baby. A nurse came in to get the baby's heart rate, but couldn't find it, so she called in an OB/GYN nurse, and she couldn't find it either. I'd just been to my doctor a week before and everything was fine.

Folks had earlier told me that this hospital was not the best one to go to. At this point, that information was the only thing keeping me from getting panicky. When the doctor came back and heard what had happened, he looked pretty disgusted, and said he'd find it himself, which he did with no problem. I walked out with two prescriptions, but can you believe one drug wasn't good to take if you're pregnant? Well, thank God the pharmacist let me know before he filled it.

At my previous visit to the doctor, I'd had a blood test that would give a percentage of your chances on having a Down syndrome child. When my doctor announced on May 22nd that my chances were 1-out-of-18, which was quite high for someone my age, I thought I would cry. I just knew this baby was going to be fine, so why did I bother having this stupid test.

She told me that I could have an amniocentesis, but there were risks of miscarrying. With my luck the baby would be normal, but I'd end up miscarrying, so I declined and requested an ultrasound instead. The ultrasound wouldn't show if the baby had Down syndrome, but it could pick up any other problems.

I tried putting the percentages out of my mind, but unfortunately now the thought was ALWAYS there. I let both sides of our family know everything that was said at the doctors, and everyone told me they'd been praying for this child and for us the whole time. I so strongly believe in prayer, and know God wouldn't give us anything we couldn't handle, so I turned to the good Lord once again and said, "It's in your hands."

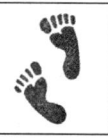

Chapter Twelve

When Clint was 11 months old he was getting fairly big to be carrying around, so we had a custom wheelchair made for him, which he seemed to like. Since it held his body straight and he sat up higher than his stroller, he could see everything better. Giving him a bath was very hard on my back, and between my pregnancy and lifting Clint all the time, I was going to the chiropractor quite often.

I decided it was time to try to get a personal care attendant to help with Clint. My niece Erin was graduating from high school in June and wanted to be a PCA, so she became Clint's aid. This worked out perfectly, especially since Clint adored Erin. Whenever she'd hold him, he'd look at her with those angelic eyes and make the cutest cooing noises to her. I was able to get the best snapshots of him whenever she was around.

Since Clint was so young, he was only eligible for 16 PCA hours. It wasn't much, but anything was helpful. My mother was a godsend too and volunteered whenever I

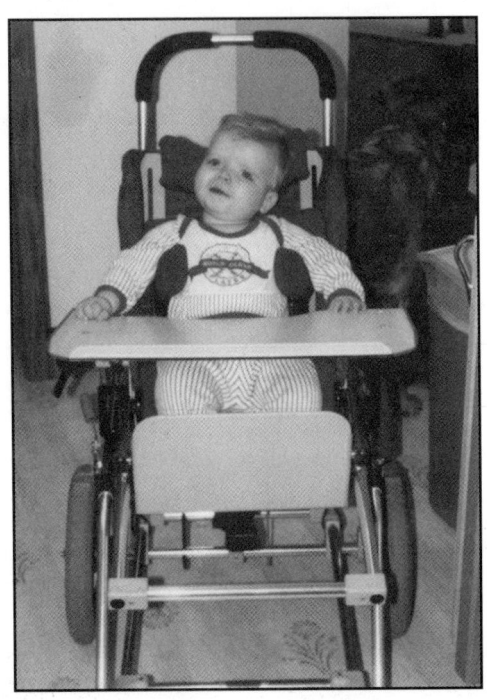

needed it. She'd take Clint overnight a couple times a week, which gave me extra time with Jesse. I was neglecting Jesse a lot. Clint took up so much time. I was extremely lucky that my family could help out. I've talked to other people with disabled children who don't have that luxury, and it's tough for them. It's sad to think in today's society people don't help each other out, causing families to rely on the government instead.

It was another hot humid summer in 1995 and I was miserable being pregnant. We couldn't afford air conditioning, so I was one fat, crabby, tired woman. Jesse was the only one who didn't seem to mind the heat. Since my parents and mother-in-law had air conditioning, we'd visit them more often than usual. It was more work than it was worth, though. Whenever I left the house, I had to pack a big diaper bag. It had to have diapers, formula, a change of clothes, and all of Clint's medicine. If we were going anywhere besides my parents house, I'd also take the wheelchair. The chair wasn't as heavy as the standard kind but it didn't fold up, so arranging it in the van became a real art form. This was another reason why I went to the chiropractor often.

I learned the hard way why most people don't bother taking their disabled child anywhere. When we did go somewhere air conditioned, I sometimes wished we hadn't. I would've been less miserable if I just stayed home and got used to the heat during the day. There was no relief for poor Clint however, and unless he stayed at my mom's he seemed

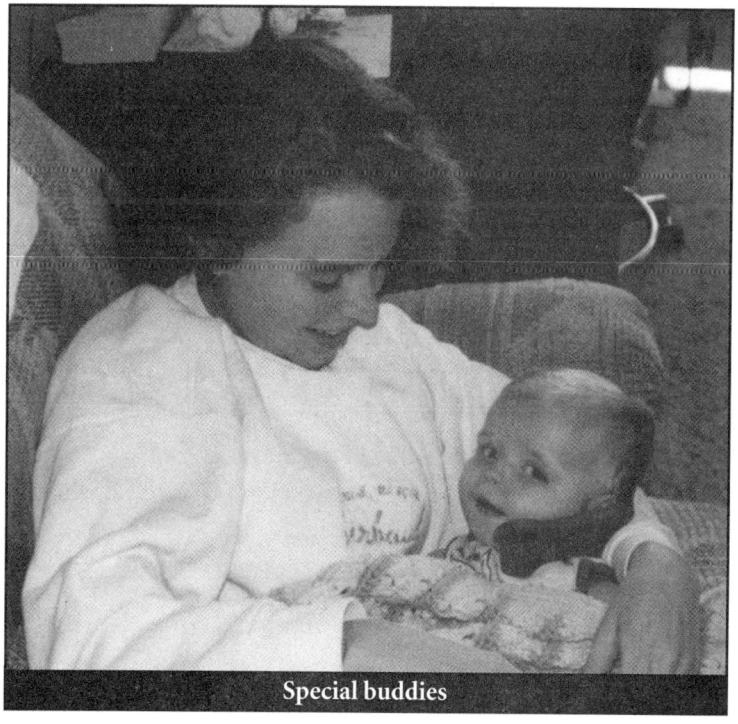

Special buddies

to suffer more than anyone else. If he liked baths, I would've done that to cool him off, but he hated them. Whenever we'd bathe him, he'd just lie there and scream and get so upset he would start to seizure. It was hard for me to let Erin bathe Clint alone. Instead of happy sounds you normally hear from a baby getting a bath, I'd hear scream, scream, silence...scream, scream, silence...(the silence came whenever he'd seizure). After awhile, Erin and I had to joke about it just to keep from crying.

On June 7th, Kurt came straight from work to meet me at the hospital for my ultrasound. The woman who was doing it had the personality of a rock. Kurt and I tried to get her to make casual conversation, but she pretty much ignored us and stared at the ultrasound screen. At the end of the test, she told us she wanted the specialist to look at something, then she left.

Kurt and I were dumbfounded. We didn't know whether to be worried about the baby or not. When the specialist and the woman came back in to look at the screen, the two of them talked medical terminology to each other, acting as if Kurt and I weren't even in the room. I was getting pretty ticked, but I tried to act calm and ask what was wrong. He told us everything was okay, she just had questions about what she saw on the placenta, and then the specialist left as quickly as he came in. Kurt and I walked out of that room more confused than ever.

I called my OB/GYN a few days later and told her what had happened. She reassured me everything was fine on the ultrasound test, and the only thing she saw was a crease on the placenta; nothing to be concerned about, but she changed my due date to November 20th. She suggested I write to the hospital and tell them what happened and what I thought of their service.

Chapter Thirteen

I decided against having a party for Clint's first birthday in June. He wouldn't be able to understand what was going on, much less appreciate presents. The little sweetie wouldn't even be able to eat his own cake. I felt depressed that day; it reminded me of the year before, when we thought he was normal, healthy. Now we wondered how many more birthdays he'd be with us?

The day after Clint's birthday I had an appointment at the funeral home. Since we were all still healthy, it seemed the best time to go. I dreaded this, but I needed to do it while my head was still clear. I didn't want to go overboard and spend a fortune due to grief. I was grateful my mother would meet me at the funeral home for moral support. My parents were friends with the mortician, so that helped break the ice.

When he brought out a little coffin for infants and set it on the table, I really thought I'd lose it. My brain went on overload as I stared at that tiny casket...Oh Lord—other people deal with this agony of losing their babies too. When he walked out of the room for a moment, I looked at the tears in Mom's eyes and knew she was thinking the same thing I was. The only thing either of us could say was, "WHEW!" We were so glad when that meeting was over, and hoped we wouldn't be back there soon.

Jesse started summer school two days a week at the end of June, and Erin helped me with Clint. I only had a few hours to myself, but it was a little bit of heaven. Some days I'd do nothing but sit at the computer and play solitaire just to relax. I knew in about five months there wouldn't be any more time to relax, so I wanted to take advantage of this while I could.

The stress of caring for both Clint and Jesse must have really been getting to me, because I'd forget things *all* the time. One day as I was talking to Mom on the phone, and sitting in my usual spot on the left side of the couch feeding Clint, Kurt asked me to do something for him outside. I asked Mom to hold on as I pushed myself with Clint up off the couch, and waddled outside. Finished, I went back, sat down on the couch and continued feeding Clint. Many minutes later, I hear BEEP, BEEP, BEEP, BEEP—in that short time I forgot I'd been on the phone! When I called her back, she obviously wasn't happy. My mother is very understanding about most stupid things I do, but this wasn't one of them. She thought I was being just plain rude. I couldn't blame her for being mad.

 # Chapter Fourteen

In May of 1995, Kurt, his brother Marty, and good friend Scott started their own antifreeze recycling business. They were up and running after the fourth of July, and because the business started out slow, Kurt and Marty kept their full-time jobs until the business grew large enough to support them. Scott quit his job to be a full-time sales and recycling employee with our company. My job was to take care of the incoming calls and do the book work. At first it was no big deal, since the calls were so few and there wasn't much bookkeeping to do. It took my mind off our problems.

On Friday, August 25th, Scott mentioned their four month old daughter Kaylen had a really bad cold and wasn't doing well. On Monday afternoon, Scott called me from a hospital saying Kaylen had died! My brain went into a fog. I heard him say something about her cold…turning into pneumonia…her heart just stopped…they'll find out more after an autopsy…I couldn't believe what I was hearing.

This wasn't supposed to happen to our friends! God this isn't right…why should they have to suffer like we've been? After cussing God out for awhile, I realized life is *not* fair.

The next few days were hard on everyone. I wanted to comfort Scott's wife Cheryl, but didn't know what to say. I was grieving for Clint, but in a different way than she was for Kaylen. Clint was still with us, so I could kiss his little chubby cheeks and forehead, but Cheryl didn't have that luxury. When Kurt talked to Scott he seemed to know exactly what to say. Kurt tried to help Scott and Cheryl think of Kaylen's death differently. He said to them, "What if they'd been able to revive her, and she had been deprived of oxygen too long causing her to be like Clint or maybe worse."

He also told them he felt Clint died the day he was diagnosed; we were just taking care of his body until it was his time to once again be with God. Kurt said he wished we could just grieve and get on with our lives. He wanted to show them that other people might have it tough and still pull through. I think that's the reason why I go to support groups. I listen to what other people have to deal with, and wonder how they cope with their problems. The funny thing is, they're thinking the same about me. I truly believe "God doesn't give you anything you can't handle." It's been true for us.

The funeral for Kaylen was difficult. They had the visitation at the same funeral home where I'd just finished making Clint's arrangements. Walking in there, knowing we'd eventually be doing this ourselves some day made my stomach queasy, but it was for Scott and Cheryl I cried that day.

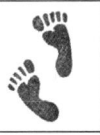 # Chapter Fifteen

Jesse doesn't like spontaneous surprises of any kind. School started for him in September and he rode on the special education bus. Jesse is fascinated with any kind of vehicle, but the noise of trucks and school buses hurt his ears. During the summer, he was able to walk around in one of the smaller buses while it sat idle, so Jesse became accustomed to it. After that first day of checking out the bus on his terms, he loved riding in it.

All we need to do is tell him what to expect ahead of time. It usually takes at least three times until he understands, then he won't throw a temper tantrum. Autistic children can have a hard time adjusting to change, but Jesse usually understands what I'm saying to him, so he's a good kid as long as he knows what's expected.

With Jesse being back in school, we knew he'd be bringing home more colds and illnesses. He had a bad habit of constantly putting his hands in his mouth, so it was inevitable he'd catch a cold as soon as school started. September and early October went well, and luckily none of us came down with any colds. But the end of October brought a different story and we all came down with a cold. I got over this one quickly, but Jesse's turned into another ear infection and had to be put back on antibiotics. Clint was having a hard time and just couldn't shake this one. It affected his lungs immediately. Clint's oxygen level began to drop and he began having a hard time swallowing, so on October 30th we had his pediatrician order an oxygen and a suction machine. We'd been faithfully suctioning out the back of his throat with a bulb syringe, but it just wasn't enough and the suction machine was able to relieve him faster.

After the machines were delivered and my mother and I were trained how to use them, Mom took Clint home with her again as she'd been doing since August. She'd take him Monday afternoons, then bring him back on Wednesday, which was a nice break for us. I had an OB/GYN appointment on Tuesday afternoon, so Mom watched both boys. When I returned, I noticed my mom was a bit nervous about Clint. She said she had to use the suction machine a lot on him the night before and was becoming concerned. I wanted to be with Clint if he died, so I told her I wanted him home with me. I knew it would be physically hard to do, but Erin would be there part of the time to help me lift him.

I was remembering a conversation back in March with a woman from the lissencephaly network. Her son had Miller-Dieker Syndrome like Clint, and died when he was two years old. The conversation we'd had at that time comforted me. She told me she didn't know if she could ever handle her son's death. Every time he got sick, she'd pray hard to help him get through it. The last time he got sick, he was hospitalized. She met a woman there who'd gone through a similar ordeal. This woman said her child, though very sick, seemed to stay alive just for her. One day, she finally gave her child permission to go be with God, and her daughter died peacefully that same night. After the conversation with this stranger, she went back to her son's room and told her husband what this woman had said.

Jesse & Clint, October 1995

By the end of the week, their own son was hooked up to monitors, and things looked pretty grim. At this time she gave her son permission to die, and she too felt at peace with this, but for some reason he still hung on. Shortly after, her husband was sitting with their sleeping son holding his hand, when she noticed her husband's eyes were closed as in sleep. Just then the monitor alarm went off indicating the boy was dying. She instantly became furious wondering how he could sleep through the death warning of their son, when her husband opened his eyes and said, "I had just given him permission to leave us."

I found myself often thinking about that story. Part of me wanted to believe Clint would get better, yet at the same time I wanted this whole ordeal to be finished. Every morning I'd pray for God to give me the strength to make it through the day. Each morning I'd wake up and wonder as I walked towards Clint's room, would I find a lifeless little boy in that crib? My baby was due soon and Clint still wasn't getting any better, so my other fear was that I'd go into labor with my mom taking care of the boys, and Clint would die at their house without me being there.

On November 15th, Erin and I brought both boys to the pediatricians. Jesse for his ear infection, and Clint was breathing terribly fast, almost to the point of panting. His heart rate had also been fast for the past two weeks. The doctor checked his oxygen level and it was only at 76 percent. The look on the doctor and nurse's faces was enough to tell me, he was not going to be getting any better. We took him home and put him on oxygen full-time.

I went to a support group that night after the boys went to bed. The only people at the support group were the coordinator, her trainee and me. I was glad it was just the three of us since my tears flowed freely, and I was able to pour my heart out to them. I remember saying, "I must be out of my mind, having such a sick child and the next baby is due in only five days. I don't know if I can handle all this. Why did I get pregnant? What were we thinking! I must be nuts!"

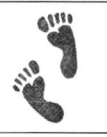 # Chapter Sixteen

The next morning, November 16th, Jesse still wasn't feeling well and had diarrhea from the antibiotics. I kept him home from school, and told Erin to come after 1:00 instead of her usual morning time. I was hoping everyone would sleep late, but no such luck.

I began my typical daily routine: dress Jesse, get his breakfast ready, start a video for him so I could get Clint's bottle and medicine. I decided to leave Clint in his pajamas, as Erin would bathe him later. Bringing Clint downstairs, we settled into our usual spot on the couch, then I gave him his phenobarbital and depakene in the syringe. For several days he'd been getting too weak to suck from a bottle, so with the syringe I would slowly dribble milk into the side of his mouth so he wouldn't choke. As I looked at his sweet little face, it just tore me up inside. He was so miserable trapped in that little body, I couldn't stand seeing him suffer. Then suddenly that conversation in March came to mind.

I looked into those big blue eyes and said, "It's okay to go to the light. You'll be with God and you'll be free. Free of this yucky medicine and free of this body that doesn't work right. You can come visit me, daddy and Jesse anytime. I love you sweet baby Clint, and it's okay to go to that beautiful bright light now."

I was crying openly as I said this, but felt totally at peace. Clint lay quietly with his eyes half open and kept taking the milk I was giving him. He was half done with his bottle, which made me happy that he was able to drink that much, when all of a sudden he made a strange gurgling noise and began spitting up. I quickly sat him up straight, wiped his nose and mouth, and was about to pat his back when I noticed he was totally still. Examining his face, the bluish tinge around his eyes and mouth were now gone. Instead he had a beautiful china doll coloring. I noticed then that the vein on his neck that had been pulsing so hard and fast was completely still.

"Clint?" I said softly.

Silence.

Oh my God, is this it, I thought? It must be...he looks so peaceful. Please God help me! What do I do now? Who do I call first...Kurt? The funeral home? The pediatricians? Dr. Dobyns? My mind was racing. Yes, Dr. Dobyns...he'll know what to do. I called the university and told them it was an emergency, so of course they put me on hold! While waiting, I ran upstairs to find the paper work I'd gotten from the funeral home. I didn't want to put Clint down, but needed both hands to look for the papers.

I carefully placed him on the bed for a few seconds, grabbed the papers, then scooped him back up into my arms.

When the woman from the university returned to the phone, she said with apologies that Dr. Dobyns was on his rounds and wasn't answering his pager. By this time I was beginning to come unglued and said, "My son just died. Can't you put a 911 on his pager or something?" She replied again that there was nothing she could do if he didn't answer his pager, so I told her to have him call me ASAP.

I paged Kurt, then called Robin. I was so grateful that they lived next door, as I needed so much to be with someone.

I sat down on the couch with the phone in one hand and Clint in the other, and called my parents. When my dad answered, he started to cry when I told him; that made me finally begin crying too. He said mom had gone to the doctor, but he'd contact her at the clinic. Next I called Erin and asked her to call her mom for me, then I called my mother-in-law, and she in turn called the relatives.

Somebody more official needed to know about Clint, I reasoned, so I contacted the pediatricians next, who told me no one had ever pronounced a death before, so maybe I should call the funeral home, which I did. They replied they didn't do that either, but they'd notify the county sheriff for me. I couldn't believe this was happening! What kind of rinkydink city did I live in where nobody would come out to pronounce the death of a child?

All of a sudden Jesse ran up to us, leaned on me, and put his face right up to Clint's. He quickly smiled at him, then he jumped back down and ran upstairs to resume his playing. The odd thing about this is that Jesse had never really paid much attention to his brother before. I wondered what was going through his mind. How I wished he was able to tell me.

Immediately after this, Robin and her two girls walked in the door, and Kurt returned his page. Finally I was able to have someone with me—especially those two girls to help keep Jesse occupied for awhile.

When the sheriff arrived at our house, both sides of the family were all there. He walked in the door, looked around the room and remarked, "This death looks suspicious." I started to tell him about Clint, then turned around and grabbed the DNR letter which was taped next to the phone. He glanced at it briefly and said it still looked suspicious, so he'd have to call out the investigation unit. I got a vision of our family splashed across front page news with charges of child abuse or neglect! Now I wish we'd received hospice like my father-in-law.

Well, lucky for us the investigation unit had contacted our pediatrician while enroute to our house, so everything was explained to them. They apologized as they walked through our door, "We wouldn't have come had we known the whole story ahead of time." Turning to Kurt, they asked only a few questions, took a couple of pictures of Clint, then they left.

Shortly after that, Dr. Dobyns showed up and explained all this was merely a formality for the death certificate. He asked if I knew the exact time Clint died? When I replied it was about 9:30 this morning, I glanced at my watch and was astonished to find it was after one p.m...I had been carrying Clint around for over three hours! Occasionally I had allowed other family members to hold him too, but only briefly. I didn't want to let go of him, now that he was so peaceful.

Dr. Dobyns didn't stay long, since he'd had to juggle appointments to come. He gave me a hug, and told me to let him know later the details about the funeral. Knowing how busy he is at the university, I was impressed that he took the time to drive to our house—a 35 mile trip one way—and assure us he'd be there for Clint's funeral. But this was just another example of the man's compassion throughout our boy's life. We couldn't have asked for a better doctor.

Clint was upstairs in his crib when the funeral director arrived. When he asked us what day we wanted to have the funeral, we agreed to have it on Saturday since my due date for the next baby was in four days. This was very short notice for everyone, but I was afraid the stress of all of this might put me into labor.

The director, Kurt and I went upstairs to get the little body. As he covered his face with the blanket, it really hit me this time—Clint was dead, and this guy was going to take away my baby! He carried the lifeless bundle out to his car; we followed him and watched as he laid Clint's body down in the back seat. This was almost more than I could handle, so to stifle a sob I joked, "What—you mean you're not gonna put him in a car seat?" The poor man turned to me with a horrified look on his face, then I said quietly, "Look…if I don't laugh about this, I'll start crying." But I could no longer hold back as Kurt and I held each other and watched him drive away with our baby Clint.

Since we had an appointment at the funeral home in an hour and a half, everyone left soon after they helped us with the newspaper notice. My parents took Jesse with them, and Mom asked if they should keep him overnight. I thanked her for the offer, but felt it was probably confusing enough for the boy, and we wanted him to be with us and make it normal as possible for him.

When we got home I wasn't hungry, so I made a frozen pizza for Kurt and Jesse. As I was cleaning up the few supper dishes, I noticed the counter was still full of Clint's medicine. I began frantically, joyously throwing his stuff out while talking to Clint, "You're free! Free of all this awful tasting medicine you hated so much! Free of those horrendous, uncontrollable seizures! Free, free...*free* at last!"

That's when I realized that all my prayers for Clint had been answered. I'd wanted to be with him when he died, and I was. My sweet boy died knowing he was loved right up to the end! And how remarkable that he left us right before this next baby was to arrive. Had this all been part of some mysterious universal plan? I thought once more of the big smile Jesse had given to Clint right after he died. What did he know about Clint that I didn't?

# Chapter Seventeen

The next day was Friday and I only had this day to get everything in order for the funeral on Saturday morning. I called Cheryl and asked if it wouldn't be too difficult for her if she could help me. She said she'd be glad to and came over with some things. We put a picture collage together, some poems, and some music choices. I thank God for her that day. I don't know how I would've been able to do it without her. We did a lot of crying, but it was very therapeutic for both of us.

After the funeral, I planned on putting the collage of pictures to the left of the window where Clint's crib was, and the cross I received from my mother-in-law was to go on the right. As I was showing Cheryl, I noticed the cross was missing from the wall. I looked in the crib, and there it was lying face down. Examining the nail where it had been hanging, I could tell the cross would've had to be carefully lifted up over the head of the nail to come off the wall. Cheryl appeared puzzled as I was. At first I thought maybe Jesse got in the crib and took it off the wall, but there was too much stuff in the crib and nothing had been moved around.

Saturday morning when I was getting ready for the funeral and drying my hair, there was a sudden strong odor that smelled exactly like Clint. I moved back slightly and couldn't smell it anymore. I moved up again and could smell it like the moment before. It only lasted seconds, but it was very comforting and I felt more relaxed when we left for the funeral home.

The service is but a blur to me now. I only remember bits and pieces, like bursting into tears to someone that I wasn't even close to, and the words to one of the special songs I'd chosen were hard to understand. That was disappointing, because I wanted everyone to hear it. I'm sure not one other person noticed these things except me.

Sunday afternoon I decided to take apart Clint's crib to make room for the new baby. I took the sheets off the mattress and pulled the mattress out of the crib. Since Clint's crib was already old and rickety, we planned to destroy it. When I walked downstairs to wash the sheets, Clint's scent was still a part of them, and I started crying again. As Kurt hugged me he asked, "Why do you do these things to yourself? I could've taken the crib down for you." I said I knew that, but I needed to keep myself busy. Kurt just shook his head and mumbled something about finding happier things to do, to keep myself busy.

Sunday night another strange thing happened. We have a double light switch in our bedroom, one for the ceiling fan, and the other for a light.

The fan itself hadn't worked for over a year, but the light functioned just fine. I was getting ready for bed and Kurt was already settled in, when I headed for the bathroom and noticed one of the switches was on. Puzzled because it was dark in the room, I turned around to see if it was the light or the fan. Just as I looked up, the fan started to move! Neither Kurt nor I had turned that switch on, and the fan hasn't worked since, no matter how we've tried to get it going.

After the fan incident so many strange things started to happen, that I decided to put them all down in my journal.

Fri. 17th—Cross fell off the wall into the crib.

Sat. 18th—Smelled Clint's scent while drying my hair.

Sun. 19th—Fan switch on & fan worked.

Mon. 20th—In the middle of the night we were awakened by a shampoo bottle falling in the bathtub.

Tues. 21st—As I was brushing my teeth, a matchbox car that had been on the back of the sink for weeks with its wheels wedged between the wall & the sink, fell down.

Wed. 22nd—Shampoo bottle fell again in the middle of the night.

When I watched that matchbox car fall by itself off the back of the sink, I exclaimed, "Well, hello Baby Clint—glad you could visit." I didn't know why any of these things were happening, so I figured it couldn't hurt to talk to Clint, especially if he was trying out those new wings of his.

Wednesday afternoon Jesse and I were playing on the bed and I looked at him and asked, "Do you miss Baby Clint? I know you can't tell me, but I wish I knew what you were thinking." Just as I said this, Jesse jumped down off the bed and left the room. Puzzled, I went to follow him and found him sitting in the new crib hugging one of Clint's stuffed animals. I stood in the doorway in disbelief and started to cry. For someone who doesn't talk well, he certainly knows how to communicate!

 # Chapter Eighteen

Thanksgiving was exactly a week after Clint died, and was also the first holiday without Clint. I was so depressed, and it started off by me glancing at my watch at 9:30 in the morning. Realizing exactly a week ago Clint died in my arms, the tears started to flow all over again.

A few days after the funeral, I started having images of Clint dying in my arms over and over again. At night, I'd have reoccurring dreams that I could save Clint from his death, by turning him upside down and squeezing his chest, so all the fluid from his lungs would clear out, and he could breathe normal again. I called Cheryl and asked if she had had strange dreams and visions. She empathetically said she had them too, but they decrease in time.

I told my family months before, that I'd probably go into labor while eating our big meal, so everyone watched me closely on Thanksgiving day. The funny thing was, my water broke 15 minutes past Thanksgiving, and I had a beautiful baby boy named Travis Joseph at 5:15 Friday morning. The roller coaster of emotions I had in those two days were incredibly overpowering.

Travis is a healthy, happy, normal little boy. Of course we watched for any signs of lissencephaly and autism, but with all the prayers from friends and family I knew he'd be okay. I'm glad we have video and pictures of him, because I don't remember much of the first four months in his life. It was as if I was taking up where I left off from Clint. I even sat in the same spot on the couch to feed him. I was so used to the way I fed Clint, that I had to stop myself from squeezing Travis' cheeks. One time as I was watching TV, Kurt said "Don't you think you should burp him?"

I looked down and noticed Travis had sucked down the whole bottle in minutes! I was so used to Clint taking over an hour to finish, that I was just thankful Travis didn't spit it all up.

Other people called Travis, Clint by mistake the first few months too. Most of them would say, "Oh my gosh, I'm so sorry!" Putting them at ease my response was always, "Oh, I do that too, *all* the time." When Travis started doing things like holding his head up, and sitting up, I could clearly see his own personality emerging, and was able to separate the two.

Travis contracted what the doctor's thought was RSV (a bronchial infection), and here we were bringing Travis to the hospital at 2 1/2 months. Kurt was surprised I was able to stay so calm as we rode together to the hospital. I told him I knew it was different this time. The hospital didn't seem too concerned, but advised us to use a nebulizer on him.

Since we had one for Clint and used it on him a lot, it was an all too familiar procedure. Of course Travis (and I) recovered from that little ordeal just fine.

I found out a few months later that my girlfriend T.J.'s new baby (who was born premature) had RSV the same time Travis did, only he had it much worse. She didn't tell me until it was all over, because she didn't want to burden me with her trivial problems. It gave her strength thinking of us and what we'd been through, compared to what was happening to them. I told her those things are *never* trivial when you're going through them, and it hurt to think my friends wouldn't talk about their problems just because they felt we had such a tragedy.

Travis was my sanity. He filled that awful void I had, not being able to hold Clint. But there were hard times when Travis took his nap, and I'd spend that time yearning for Clint. I was so used to having a house full of people when Clint was here, that when he died it all abruptly stopped and I was left totally alone. It took quite some time before I got used to a quiet house.

I felt extremely lucky when we got our computer on-line. I met the most wonderful compassionate people through Microsoft Network's parent chat rooms. I made some fantastic friends who got me through some terrible depressing days. Clint was intertwined with so many people that I felt lucky I could talk about him, but it was nice to be able to reveal my feelings and cry openly without anyone being able to see or hear me.

At the end of December, Jesse's pediatrician and I made the decision to have tubes put into his ears. He was constantly on antibiotics, which never totally cleared up the trapped fluid. That very day when the surgery was done, he started repeating whatever anyone said. It wasn't a cure-all for his autism (like I had hoped), but it certainly helped his speech come along much quicker. It was funny watching the look on his face the next day, as he plugged and unplugged his ears with his fingers. You could tell by his expression he was thinking, WOW, I used to hear like this, now I can hear better!

Jesse never went through the typical parent separation anxiety when he was a baby, instead it started a little over a month after Clint died. Jesse went to preschool twice a week, on Tuesday and Thursday mornings. Tuesday's the parents were with their children the first hour, then they'd go to a separate room and discuss parenting issues the second hour. Jesse never had a problem with me leaving before Clint died, but after the first of the year he'd cry and scream "Mama Mama," and when I'd start to leave, he clung to me so hard, the teachers had to pry him off. I reassured him that I'd be back soon, but it didn't seem to help much.

My mom speculated that he wasn't getting good care at school, since he wasn't doing that when she took care of him. Well, she spoke too soon. I had her watch Jesse one day at her house, while I took Travis for his annual check up and he screamed and sobbed just like at school. I was beginning to wonder if he thought we had just left Baby Clint somewhere and never came back for him, and maybe we'd do that to him too.

Death is so hard to understand for adults, I'd love to know what Jesse thinks about it. I explained to him what happened to Clint as best I could, but Jesse's so visual in his thoughts that I'm sure it's hard for him to grasp the concept of God and heaven, especially if he can't see it for himself.

Jesse slowly did get over his separation anxiety, but it took him over eight months. I think the memory of Clint simply faded for him once Travis got older and started moving around.

 # Chapter Nineteen

On Monday May 6, 1996 I received a phone call from my mother who was at the hospital. She said dad had a bad accident with the power saw in the garage, and cut off his finger and thumb. He was still in surgery when she called and they were trying to reattach them.

My father has been battling with Parkinson's for many years now. He doesn't have the shakes like some Parkinson's patients do, instead his body is getting stiff and slow.

I went ballistic with God and started screaming, "Haven't we been through enough yet? What else are you going to put our family through? What lessons are we supposed to learn from all this?"

Funny thing is, my dad dealt with losing his fingers and thumb better than I did. He knew it was his own fault for being in a hurry, and not acting as safely as he should have. He never blamed God, he figured it was just an accident, and those things happen when you're careless. You learn from these mistakes, then get on with your life.

I admire my dad. He handles change quite well, and seems to adapt to different situations very easily. Maybe it's his mathematical mind (he's a retired math teacher) that helps him do this, I don't know, but I wish I had that ability.

 # Chapter Twenty

June 25th (Clint's birthday) snuck up on me. I thought I could handle Clint's birthday like any other day, but that didn't happen. I was having fewer and fewer days of crying spells, so I thought I'd be okay. Instead, I found myself thinking of last year and wishing I had acknowledged his first birthday if not for him, for me. When the mail came and I received a card from Cheryl, I cried. It was nice knowing I wasn't alone in my thoughts, and that someone else knew what I was going through. I ended up making my favorite birthday cake for the rest of us and thought what the heck, If I'm going to be depressed, I might as well have chocolate cake with chocolate frosting to cheer me up.

By this time Travis was becoming a little charmer and every time we'd go to a store, he'd have to flirt with all the women walking past him, and I was finally able to enjoy myself while shopping.

In September, Jesse went to preschool three days a week instead of just two. This was great for both of us. His

Travis—Summer of 1996—Contagious smile

separation anxiety had faded, and he was talking a lot better.

By the end of September we finally got around to ordering the headstone for Clint's grave. I'd been putting it off, assuming it would be too expensive, but it wasn't that bad. Since Clint was buried next to Kurt's father, we were limited on the style and size of headstone we could have installed. It was finally put in by the end of October, and Heather said, she was planning to take off work on Nov. 16th to see the grave and Kathy wanted the family over for supper, so I thought it'd be nice to have a small memorial at the cemetery that day.

On November 7th, my sister called to tell me my girlfriend's son was in a major car accident. My stomach went right to my throat. I immediately prayed for their family, and hoped everything would be fine. Later that day I went to the hair salon Maggie owns, to find out if they'd heard anything. Her employees were about to tell me they weren't sure, when the phone rang. It was Maggie's mother calling to tell them Chevas was declared brain dead, but they needed to keep him alive so they could donate his organs.

Chevas was only 17 years old. He was in the same class with my niece, Heather and would've graduated in the spring. I couldn't believe something like this was happening to another friend of mine! I wanted to be with her right then, but knew she was probably surrounded by close family members.

It was hard for me to relate with Maggie, even though we both lost our sons. I had time to grieve while Clint was still here, and knowing his quality of life wasn't good, I wondered if it was easier losing Clint, than a person like Chevas. He had such great potential, and they were making plans for when he'd graduate.

Less than a week after Chevas' funeral was the one year anniversary of Clint's death. On November 15th for the first time in my life, I sat down and wrote a poem. I was so overwhelmed by a series of emotions, I'm sure that's what brought out the ability for me to write. It was nice to read this poem at the cemetery, since it summed up my feelings perfectly.

BABY CLINT

*I knew God put you here for a purpose
and it wasn't for you to learn
I knew you were our teacher
and that's a privilege I felt honored to earn.*

*You helped your big brother
get the care that he needs
and I learned more patience and tolerance
to help me succeed.*

*You taught your doctors things
they never would've known
You've touched everyone in some way
and because of this, we've grown.*

*You brought me closer to God
than ever I could be
and now that you are with him
your light shines through us, for everyone to see.*

*God gave us a special angel
for only a short time
and even though our hearts are breaking
God knows we'll be just fine.*

I love you for eternity my Sweet Baby Clint

Love, Mom

November 16, 1996 was a bittersweet day. After reading my poem in the rain at the cemetery and letting three balloons go, we went back to my sister's for supper. When we were done eating, I put Travis down and he took his first five steps!

 # Chapter Twenty-One

It felt good writing that poem, and after that I wrote a few articles. One for the Lissencephaly Network, one for our county, and one for the school's newsletter. Writing these articles, going to different support groups, being with my friends and family, and the wonderful people I met on the computer internet all helped me to deal with the trying times in my life.

The last few holidays have been even more enjoyable. It was fun to see Travis open his presents and watch how a normal child reacts to toys. I take absolutely nothing for granted anymore. The problems that other parents complain about with their normal kids are to me just part of the fun of having healthy ones to enjoy. I marvel at everything Jesse and Travis do. There were moments when I felt I neglected Jesse because of Clint, but I hope I'm making that up to him now. And there are times when I'm a little too overprotective than I should be with Travis, but I'm getting better.

One of the hardest things about losing a child is how other people react. Anyone with a dead child wants to talk about them, but some people don't want to bring up the subject because they're afraid we'll cry. The thing is, we're always crying—at least inside. Talking about our children and writing in our journals keeps our beautiful angels alive, and if anyone wants to ask me *anything* about my sweet baby Clint, I'm always willing to talk. I hope by talking about him it may help someone along the way too.

The day before my birthday on April 15, 1997 Travis was exactly the same age as Clint was the day he died. On my birthday, Travis was older than Clint had lived, which made it a bittersweet day.

I was able to close another chapter in my life and stop comparing Travis to Clint. Travis is a little peanut of a boy, so he's still wearing some of Clint's clothes. I think once he outgrows them I'll be able to finally close the book.

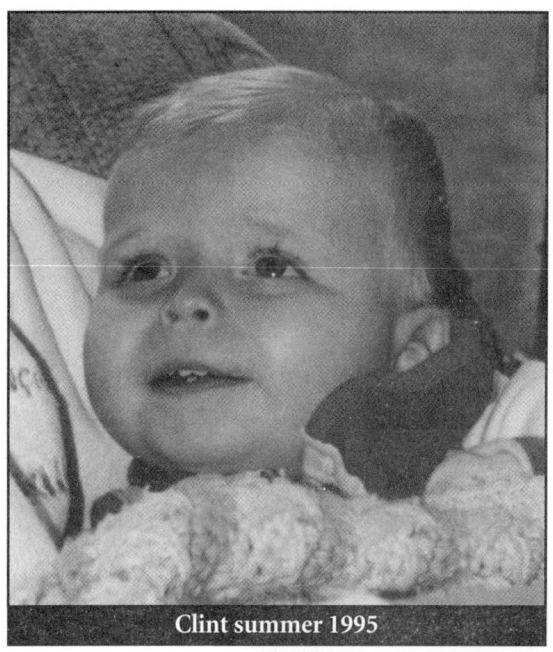

Clint summer 1995

Travis spring 1997

 # Chapter Twenty-Two

Watching Jesse and Travis interact, I realize how much I missed out on Jesse's life that year and a half while Clint was alive. Clint seemed to overshadow what Jesse did, even those wonderful temper tantrums. I was able to ignore them when he was three, but now that he's almost six, it's not so tolerable. Since Jesse *looks so normal,* there are days when I wish I could hang a sign on him saying, "I'm not a brat, I'm just autistic!"

I'll say one thing, there's never a dull moment with that boy. When I take him to the store, and don't tell him *exactly* what's expected and we don't have time to look at toys, books or magazines he'll throw himself around and scream. I'm surprised our hometown WalMart store doesn't know us on a first name basis yet.

My chiropractor has more than once shaken his finger at me for bodily picking up my 50+ pound boy and carrying him out to the car while he's kicking and screaming.

Jesse doesn't always give me trouble. He's like that old saying, "When he's good, he's very very good. When he's bad, he's horrid!" I'm just glad he's so affectionate (I've nicknamed him "huggie bug"), because it makes up for the times when he is horrid.

Some of those fun childhood experiences just don't happen with Jesse either. If it's not familiar to him, he'll cover his ears and say, "All done, all done" and run away.

One evening while eating hamburgers and popcorn for supper, Jesse was chomping on popcorn nonstop, ignoring the hamburger on his plate. I finally pushed it away and said, "No more popcorn until you eat your hamburger." He reluctantly picked up the burger and took a small bite. Seconds later I hear this loud crunch, crunch, crunch. Thinking he was chewing on a popcorn hull, Kurt and I didn't pay much attention, but when Jesse opened his mouth to take another bite from the burger, I noticed his bottom teeth, and one was missing. "Oh my gosh Kurt," I exclaimed. "He lost his first tooth...and *ate* it!"

At first I worried that he could've hurt his other teeth by chewing it up, then I wondered if it'd pass through his system okay. After his visit to the dentist (which of course he hated, and we had to hold him down, just so they could pry his mouth open), the doctor said his teeth were fine and joked that a little protein through his system wouldn't hurt him a bit. Knowing he was all right, we all had a good laugh about the toothfairy not wanting *that tooth!*

Potty training was another story in itself. Jesse had no clue about going to the bathroom until he was over five years old. We got lucky a few times, catching him going and then we'd make a big deal about it by praising him and giving him special things. The only problem was, he had no clue what he just did. Sometimes he'd get up, look at the

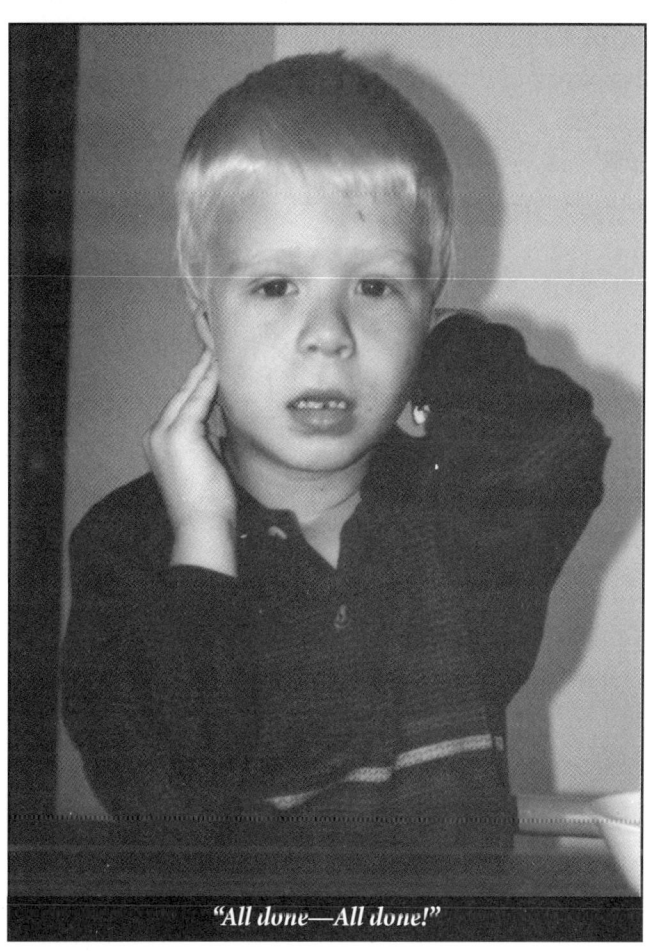

"All done—All done!"

empty toilet and clap his hands, thinking he went potty. We didn't know until later, that he wasn't aware of his body, and may not be until he's between the age of five and seven years old. When this was explained to me, my first reaction was, What? How can someone not be aware of their body?

I still don't totally understand this concept, but decided to wait until he was over five. When he started kindergarten, the special education teachers helped with his potty training and after many trial and errors, Jesse realized by using the bathroom properly he got to do his favorite thing of all time—play on the computer. He's totally potty trained now, but because of his marathon potty-training, Kurt and I joked for awhile that he'd be 16 years old, and right before he leaves for his first date we'd stop him and change his diaper.

 # Chapter Twenty-Three

People tell me experiences like these will make you stronger and I can honestly tell you, I don't know. What I do know is I'm a little wiser, tolerant, patient and have a lot more empathy than ever before. I feel we're all put on this earth for a purpose, that everyone of us are students and teachers. We all must grow mentally and emotionally at our own ability, before we go to the next level of existence.

I look at the little things that used to bother me and now think they were so trivial. Life is just too short to waste your time and energy on them. None of us knows when it's our time to die, but I certainly want to help many people and make as much of a good impact as possible before I go. I hope by telling this story about reaching out to a higher power, you can receive enough strength to get you through things you could never imagine possible.

I thank the good Lord for sending us three of his beautiful, special angels. They taught us so much in such a short time, and we're still learning from each of them every day.

Grief doesn't just magically go away. It fades away so slowly, you think it will never end, which it doesn't...not totally. But I look at myself now and see I'm making the most out of my life...my life after grief.

Travis & Jesse—September 1997

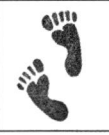# Appendix

The following information has been provided by:

> Dr. William B. Dobyns
> Neurology Department, University of MN
> Box 486, Mayo Memorial Bldg.,
> 420 Delaware St. NE
> Minneapolis, MN 55455

What is lissencephaly?

Lissencephaly is a malformation of the brain in which the brain surface is smooth rather than convoluted. The name comes from the Greek words "lissos" which means smooth and "enkephalos" which means brain.

In man, the surface of the brain is formed by a complex series if ridges and valleys. The ridges are called gyri or convolutions, and the valleys are called sulci. In children with lissencephaly, the normal convolutions are absent or only partly formed, so the surface is smooth as shown in Figure 1 on the following page.

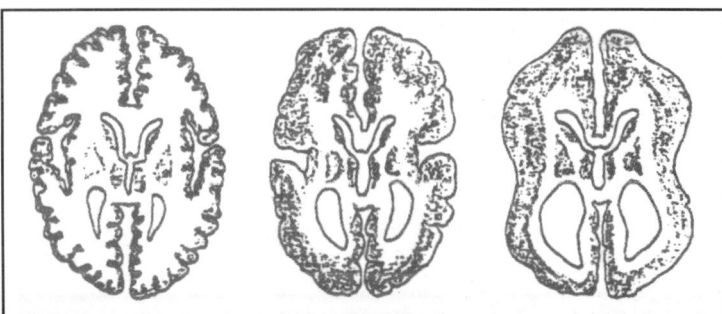

Figure 1: Drawings of brains showing a normal surface (left), mild lissencephaly or pachygyria (middle) and severe lissencephaly or agyria (right).

Lissencephaly is usually diagnosed based on interpretation of either CT or MRI scan of the brain. It can be suspected based on ultrasound in newborn children. Several other brain abnormalities occur secondary to the lissencephaly.

How does it occur?

When the brain forms during the first month of pregnancy, all the nerve cells are located in the center surrounding a fluid-filled cavity called the central canal. During the second month, support cells begin to send branches up to the surface of the brain. During the third and fourth months, the nerve cells climb up these branches to reach the surface. Each wave of nerve cells climbs above the preceding waves so that the last wave of cells is closest to the surface.

Normally, a large majority of all nerve cells are located at or just under the surface in an area called the cortex. In lissencephaly, many of the nerve cells do not reach the surface. They are stuck in an abnormal position, and so cannot make their usual connections with other nerve cells.

Are there different types?

Several different types have been described. The most common is classical or type I lissencephaly. Another is called type II lissencephaly because the appearance is so different. Patients with type II have other birth defects of the brain and eye, and most have hydrocephalus. Several other unusual types exist but all are very rare (e.g. "cerebro-cerebellar" lissencephaly and an atypical type seen in NeuLaxova syndrome).

Each of these types may occur in several different syndromes. Type I lissencephaly sequence, in Miller-Dieker syndrome and in a very rare condition called Norman-Roberts syndrome. Type II occurs in Fukuyama syndrome is usually known as Fukuyama congenital muscular dystrophy.

What will the child be like?

All children with lissencephaly have severe mental retardation and poor control of movement similar to children with cerebral palsy. Still, some do make limited developmental progress. Other common problems include poor feeding, frequent seizures and repeated episodes of pneumonia. Some differences exist between the different syndromes.

What was the cause?

Just a few years ago, lissencephaly was thought to be a genetic disorder which was inherited as a recessive trait. The data on which this decision was based later turned out to be in error. Based on my studies over the past 8 years, I believe that several different causes exist, both genetic and non-genetic.

Among these are (1) viral infections of the baby during the first trimester, (2) insufficient blood supply to the brain during the first trimester, (3) a genetic disorder with recessive inheritance, and (4) damage or mutation to a specific genetic region on chromosome 17. Other causes which have not yet been identified are likely as well.

Lissencephaly Syndromes

Several different diseases or "syndromes" with lissencephaly have been recognized. The three most common are Isolated Lissencephaly Sequence (ILS), Miller-Dieker syndrome (MDS) and Walker-Warburg syndrome (WWS). ILS includes children with lissencephaly as the major and usually the only birth defect. MDS and WWS are genetic syndromes which may be recognized based on a specific combination of birth defects.

Seizures

Most children have seizures which begin during the first year of life, although usually not during the first couple of months. Several different types of seizures may occur. Tonic seizures consist of sudden stiffening, usually of the whole body. They usually last only a few moments but can last over a minute. No further jerks are seen. However, brief tonic seizures (each lasting only a few seconds) may occur one after another over a period of many minutes. Tonic-clonic or "grand mal" seizures consist of stiffening of the body and rhythmic jerks of the head, arms and legs. These sometimes involve only part of the body. This type of seizure most often begins after the first year of life. Staring spells consist of open and unmoving eyes with a blank facial expression. These usually last only a few seconds although longer spells are possible. Small movements such as eyelid fluttering or chewing movements sometimes occur.

These seizures can usually be controlled with antiseizure medications, although 100% control is not often achieved. Because of the mixed types of seizures which occur, certain medications are more likely to be effective than others. Effectiveness of any given medication may differ between children.

In many children, the most effective medication is valproic acid (Depakene or Depakote). The second is often clonazepan (Klonopin). Other medicines such as Phenobarbital, phenytoin (Dilantin), carbamazepine (Tegretol) and ethosuximide (Zarontin) may be helpful in some children.

Some children have a severe seizure type known as infantile spasms or jackknife seizures which do not respond to the usual seizure medicines. This type of seizure occurs only in young children, usually between about 3 and 12 months of age.

They consist of a cluster of very brief but hard jerks of the whole body. The direction may be either forward or backwards. That is, some children will jerk forward with their head bent down and their legs pulled up. Others will arch their head and back backwards with the legs straightened. Each jerk lasts only a few seconds after which they relax till the next jerk. Clusters of infantile spasms may last from a few seconds to several minutes. They are most often seen just after awakening from sleep.

The most effective treatment is ACTH shots which stimulate the body to produce cortisone. Prednisone is a man-made drug which resembles cortisone. It may also be effective. Other medicines which work are valproic acid and clonazepam. Other seizure medicines are much less likely to be effective. If left untreated, infantile spasms will increase in frequency and may result in loss of any developmental abilities. Eventually, they will change to other seizure types.

(written March 1991)

Signs and Symptoms of Autism

1. Has difficulty mixing with other children

2. Acts deaf

3. Resists learning

4. Has no fear of real dangers

5. Giggles and laughs inappropriately

6. Is markedly overactive

7. Resists change in routine

8. Indicates needs by gesture

9. Is not cuddly

10. Avoids eye contact

11. Manifests inappropriate attachment to objects

12. Spins objects

13. Plays intently for abnormally long periods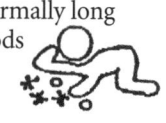

14. Has standoffish manner

For further information or to make a contribution,
please contact:

The Lissencephaly Network, Inc.
Attn: Dianna Fitzgerald
716 Autumn Ridge Lane
Fort Wayne, IN 46804
Phone or Fax: (219) 432-4310
Or visit the world wide web at : www.lissencephaly.org/

Or for more information on Autism call:

The Autism Society of America
1-800-3AUTISM

Or visit their new website at: www.autism.com/ari

or

The Autism Resource Network
5123 Westmill Road
Minnetonka, MN 55345
(612) 988-0088
Fax (612) 988-0099

Order Form

If you are not able to find *Life After Grief* at your local bookstore and would like to order more books, you may send this form with a check or money order payable to Life After Grief for $9.95 + $2.00 shipping per book to:

LIFE AFTER GRIEF
PO BOX 54
HUGO, MN 55038

Name: _____

Address: _____

City: _____ State: _____ Zip:_____

Telephone: (   ) _____

# of Books: _____   Shipping: _____

MN Residents add $0.65 sales tax per book: _____

Total: _____

If you're sending this as a gift and/or would like me to sign the book, feel free to write a brief message on the lines below.

_____

_____

_____

_____

_____

A portion of the proceeds will go to The Lissencephaly Network, The Autism Resource Network, Compassionate Friends, ARC Suburban of Washington County, and Family Service St. Croix, all of whom helped me and my family both physically and emotionally.